ENGINEERING WONDERS OF THE 21ST CENTURY

Great SPACESHIP Designs

BY SOPHIE WASHBURNE

Cavendish Square
NEW YORK

Published in 2023 by Cavendish Square Publishing, LLC
29 East 21st Street, New York, NY 10010

Website: cavendishsq.com

Cataloging-in-Publication Data
Names: Washburne, Sophie.
Title: Great spaceship designs / Sophie Washburne.
Description: New York : Cavendish Square, 2023. | Series: Engineering wonders of the 21st century | Includes glossary and index.
Identifiers: ISBN 9781502665188 (pbk.) | ISBN 9781502665195 (library bound) | ISBN 9781502665201 (ebook)
Subjects: LCSH: Space vehicles--Design and construction--Juvenile literature. | Aerospace engineering--Juvenile literature.
Classification: LCC TL875.W37 2023 | DDC 629.47'4--dc23

Editor: Jennifer Lombardo
Copyeditor: Michelle Denton
Designer: Rachel Rising

The photographs in this book are used by permission and through the courtesy of: Cover Oranzy Photography/ Shutterstock.com; cover, pp. 1–48 (gears) Artistdesign29/Shutterstock.com; cover, pp. 1–48 (grid) Cesar Termulo Jr/Shutterstock.com; pp. 1–48 (boxes) Olessia_Art/Shutterstock.com; p. 4 Allexxandar/ Shutterstock.com; p. 6 Photo 12/A7A collection/Alamy Stock Photo; p. 7 VLADJ55/Shutterstock.com; p. 8 Everett Collection/Shutterstock.com; p. 10 Rodichev Vitalii/Shutterstock.com; p. 12 Asetta/Shutterstock.com; p. 13 Alones/Shutterstock.com; p. 14 Vera Larina/Shutterstock.com; p. 16 andreyphoto63/ Shutterstock.com; p. 18 VectorMine/Shutterstock.com; p. 20 YMZK-Photo/ Shutterstock.com; p. 21 travelview/Shutterstock.com; p. 23 NASA Photo/Alamy Stock Photo; p. 25 Frame Stock Footage/Shutterstock.com; p. 26 (top) Dimitrios Karamitros/Shutterstock.com; p. 26 (bottom) AleksandrMorrisovich/Shutterstock.com; p. 28 https://commons.wikimedia.org/wiki/File:Deep_Space_1_clean_(PIA04242).png; p. 30 Dima Zel/Shutterstock.com; p. 32 Raymond Cassel/Shutterstock.com; p. 34 https://commons.wikimedia.org/wiki/File:WhippleShield.jpg; p. 36 muratart/Shutterstock.com; p. 38 SpaceX/Alamy Stock Photo; p. 39 https://commons.wikimedia.org/wiki/File:Orion_Service_Module.jpg; p. 43 https://commons.wikimedia.org/wiki/File:Bussard_Interstellar_Ramjet_Engine.jpg.

CPSIA compliance information: Batch #CSCSQ23: For further information contact Cavendish Square Publishing LLC, New York, New York, at 1-877-980-4450.

Printed in the United States of America

CONTENTS

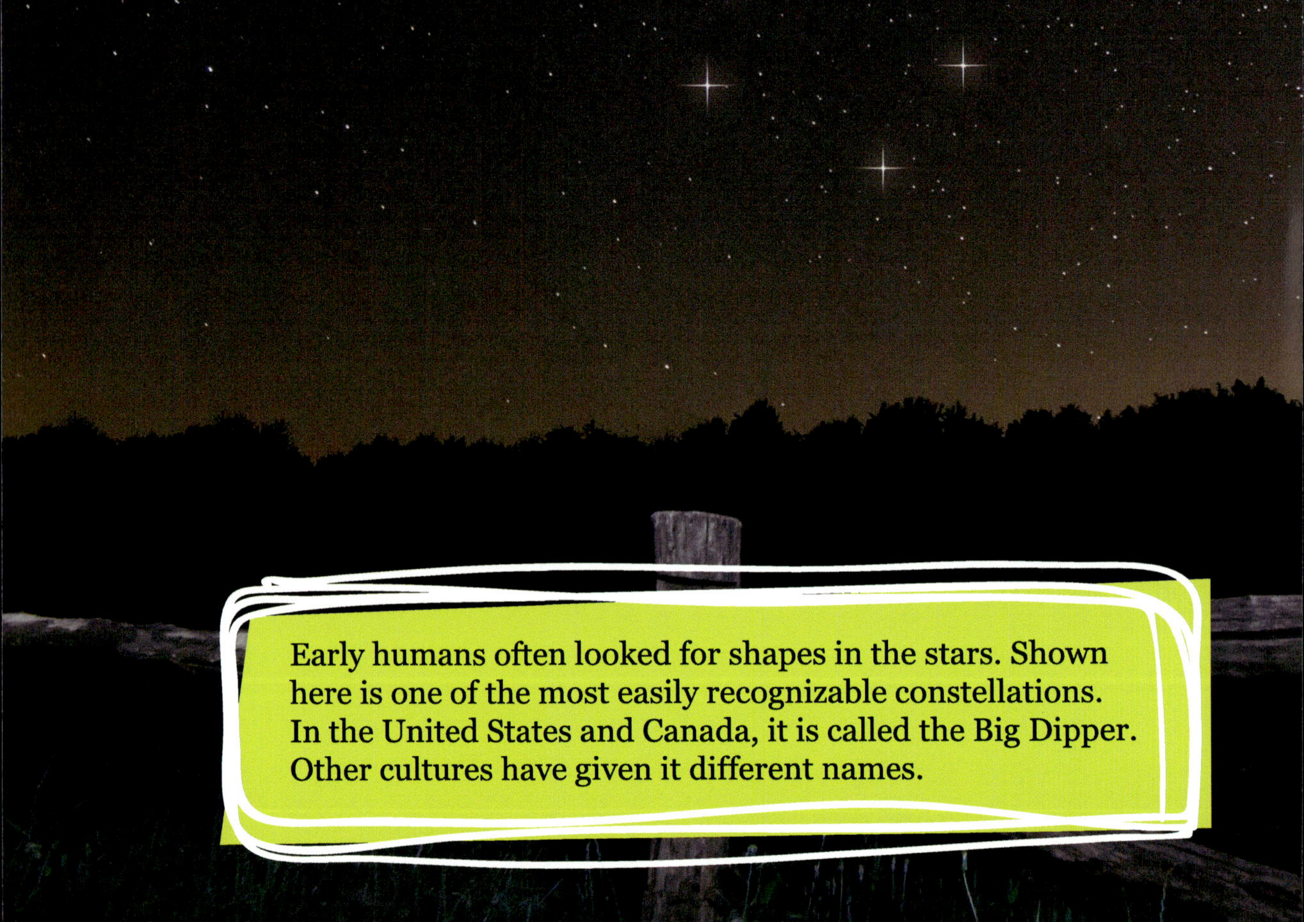

Early humans often looked for shapes in the stars. Shown here is one of the most easily recognizable constellations. In the United States and Canada, it is called the Big Dipper. Other cultures have given it different names.

Introduction

For hundreds of years, people have wondered about what space holds. Ancient civilizations used the sun and moon to create accurate calendars, and they often made up stories about the constellations, or pictures they saw in the stars. Astronomers created telescopes to get a closer look at planets such as Mars and Venus.

The imagination of science fiction often creates a starting point for scientists, and many of the things people have written about in novels have ended up becoming reality. Science fiction writers imagined a future where people traveled to and lived in outer space. For example, in 1865, Jules Verne wrote a book called *From the Earth to the Moon: A Direct Route in 97 Hours, 20 Minutes*. It was about a group of gun enthusiasts who built a weapon large enough to shoot them into space. In 1950, Ray Bradbury published *The Martian Chronicles*, which contains stories about astronauts landing on Mars and creating a new home for the people of Earth.

Shown here is a scene from the 1979 movie version of *The Martian Chronicles*. It shows an astronaut (*left*) meeting a Martian (*right*) with a Martian city in the background.

It was not until the middle of the 20th century that technology had advanced enough to build vessels that would let people actually travel to space, not just look at it from the ground. However, that technology built on inventions from the past. Between the 10th century and the 12th century CE, the Chinese invented gunpowder, which they used to power rockets. These rockets could be used as weapons to shoot at an enemy. With a slightly different design, they could also be used as fireworks. In 1903, a Russian mathematician named Konstantin Tsiolkovsky used his knowledge of math and physics to understand how rockets worked. He created a formula to explain it. This formula was named after him and remains a key part of rocket engineering today.

It is one thing to shoot an object into space, but it is quite another to send a ship full of passengers up there and keep them safe for the entire journey. Engineers have had to answer all kinds of questions to make effective spacecraft. What kinds of fuel will it take to travel into space, and where will they store it? How can they make the ships lighter and faster? What about the danger from orbiting satellites or meteorites? How will they make room for cargo and travelers? How will ships be able to land on another planet? How will they get back to Earth? If any of these or many other problems are not solved before a spaceship leaves Earth, tragedy can occur.

This statue of Tsiolkovsky can be seen in Moscow, Russia.

After the first successful launch of the V-2 rocket into space in 1946, the U.S. Army continued to do tests and improve the design. Shown here is the V-2 taking off in 1950.

CHAPTER ONE

From Rockets to Space Stations

In addition to Konstantin Tsiolkovsky, two other scientists—Hermann Oberth of Germany and Robert Goddard of the United States—became famous for their work on space rockets. All three realized certain important facts about how rockets would need to work. For example, they would need liquid fuel instead of coal or natural gas. Because there is no evidence that any of the three of them knew about each other's work, they all share the title of "Father of Rocketry."

THE SPACE RACE

During World War II (1939–1945), the Germans created rockets to use as weapons. After the war, the U.S. Army brought several German rocket scientists to America to continue their work. They rebuilt this kind of rocket, which was called the V-2, with parts they brought with them from Germany.

They successfully launched a rocket into space on May 10, 1946. The boundary between Earth and outer space is an imaginary line 62 miles (100 kilometers) above sea level. It is called the Kármán line. The rocket the U.S. Army launched traveled 71 miles (114 km).

At the same time, the government of Russia—then called the Union of Soviet Socialist Republics (USSR), or simply the Soviet Union—was also looking into rocket technology. In 1957,

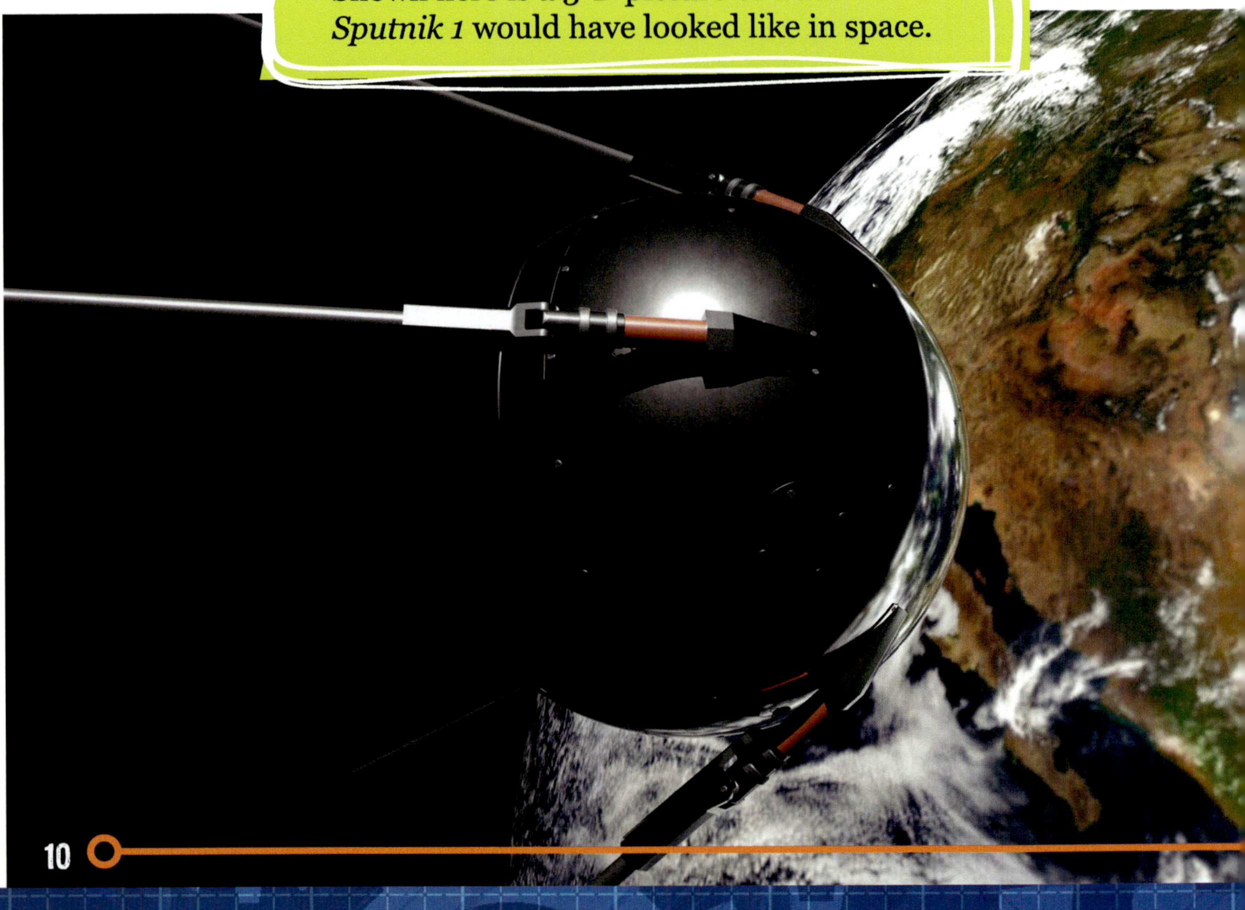

Shown here is a 3-D picture of what *Sputnik 1* would have looked like in space.

The Women Who Changed History

Most of the credit for the American rocket program has historically gone to white men. However, they never would have succeeded if not for the Black women working behind the scenes. They worked for a government organization called the National Advisory Committee for Aeronautics (NACA), which existed before the National Aeronautics and Space Administration (NASA) was formed. At the time, the organization was segregated, so Black and white employees were kept separate, as were men and women. The West Area Computing Unit was where the Black female employees worked.

The job of these black women was to analyze data and provide detailed mathematical formulas that would launch the rockets successfully. Without them, it would have been impossible for the space program to succeed. In 2016, a movie called *Hidden Figures* was released. It focused on these Black female mathematicians, especially Katherine Johnson, Dorothy Vaughan, and Mary Jackson. The movie detailed the work they did for the space program, as well as the discrimination they faced from their white male coworkers. The movie was based on a book of the same name by Margot Lee Shetterly.

they successfully launched the world's first satellite, called *Sputnik 1*, into orbit. This set off what is now known as the Space Race. The Americans were worried that the Soviets would gain military control of space if they could launch a real spaceship, so they started working harder to try to beat them there.

Before Russia and the United States sent people to space, they sent animals. The first true cosmonaut was a dog named Laika, who died in space. This statue of her can be seen in Moscow.

The Soviet Union won the first leg of the Space Race by a few weeks. The Soviet cosmonaut (the Russian term for an astronaut) Yuri Gagarin became the first man to go into space on April 12, 1961. The United States successfully launched astronaut Alan Shepard into space just 23 days later, and American John Glenn became the first man to orbit Earth in 1962.

The race heated up even more as the Soviet Union and the United States made plans to put a man on the moon. It would mean not only leaving Earth's surface, but also leaving Earth's orbit. It would require a different kind of design for fuel capacity and power as well as for a manned **capsule** and a lunar **module** to travel on the moon's surface. They would also need a way to return the astronauts to Earth.

This time, the United States came out ahead. In July 1969, the first manned spacecraft, *Apollo 11*, landed on the moon. It made history with Neil Armstrong's walk on the moon's surface and brought all three astronauts safely back home. Another 17 Apollo missions followed between 1969 and 1972.

However, the cost of fuel and spaceships was high. Every time another spacecraft was launched, the rockets fell back into Earth's atmosphere and burned up. Upon reentry, all components except the command modules were destroyed in the atmosphere. What was needed was a spaceship that could be used more than once. The solution was the invention of the space shuttle. It would not only fly into orbit, it would

The space shuttle (*shown here*) changed space travel forever.

also return to Earth and land the way an airplane does on a runway. It could also be reused for future flights.

Engineer Maxime Faget, along with many other NASA engineers, contributed years of work to the space shuttle's development. It was finally launched in 1981. During its

A Soyuz rocket such as the one shown here can carry astronauts to and from the ISS.

30-year history, a fleet of 5 different space shuttles flew a total of 135 missions. The last space shuttle was retired in 2011. During the same time period, Russia developed a series of spacecraft named Soyuz. It was designed to carry crews and cargo into space. This style of spacecraft is still in use. In fact, it is still one of the only ways for astronauts to get to the International Space Station (ISS).

For many years, Russia and the United States were competitors in the Space Race. However, in the 1990s, they began working together. In 1998, the two countries, along with agencies from 15 others, began to build the ISS. By the end of the 20th century, the ISS was ready for its first crew.

THINK IT THROUGH

1. Why would a rocket need liquid fuel instead of solid or gas?
2. Why do we need the Kármán line?
3. Why does a manned spacecraft need a different design than an unmanned one?

It takes a lot of power to get a spaceship off the ground. That is why this rocket has so many openings for burned fuel to escape and push it off the ground.

CHAPTER TWO

Understanding Physics

It takes a lot of science to get a spacecraft off the ground, into orbit, and safely back down to Earth. Engineers need to think about how to overcome gravity, how to protect the crew from heat and radiation, and how to make the spacecraft land safely after its high-speed reentry through the atmosphere.

LEAVING EARTH

For a spacecraft to launch off the planet, it must have enough power to escape Earth's gravity. To manage that, it needs two things: thrust and speed. Thrust is based on Sir Isaac Newton's principle that every action has an equal and opposite reaction. For example, if a person blows up a balloon and then lets it go, the air will shoot out toward them and push the balloon in the opposite direction. A rocket engine works the same way. As the fuel burns up inside the rocket, it turns into a

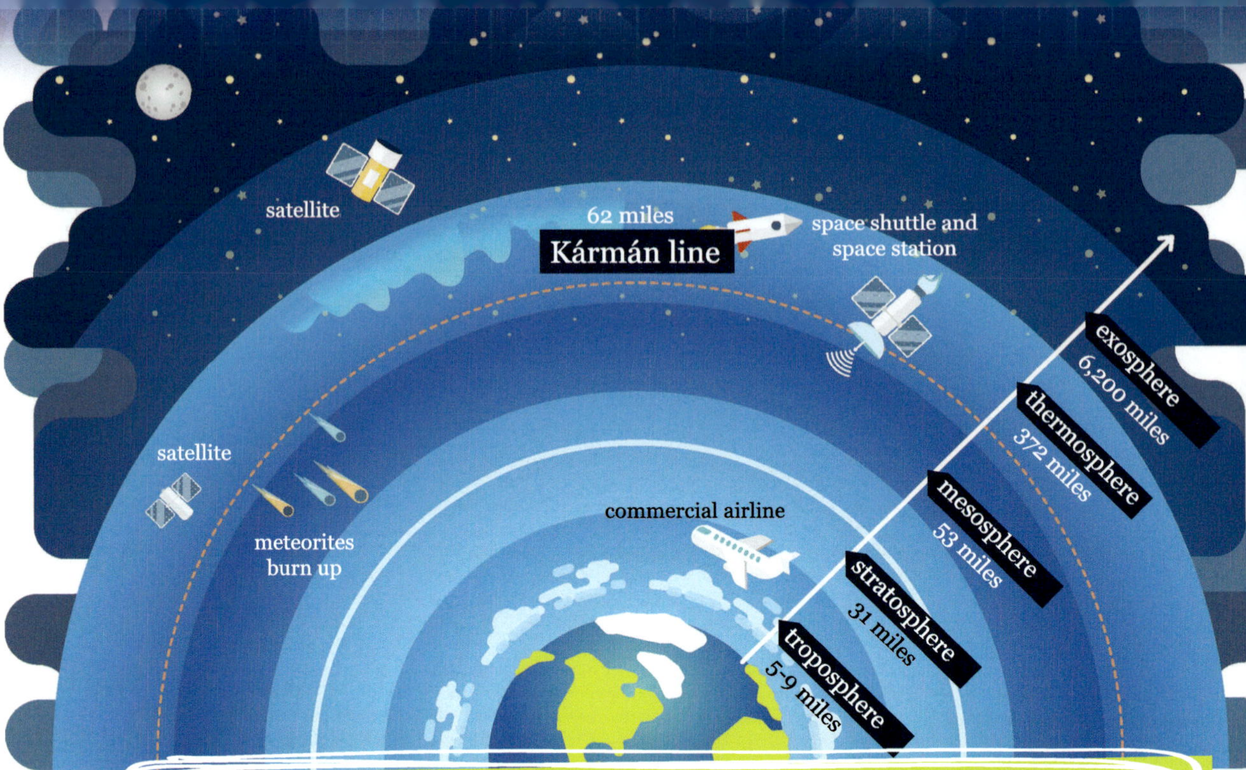

This diagram shows the layers of Earth's atmosphere. The Kármán line is the point at which the atmosphere turns into outer space.

gas that pushes out toward Earth, which thrusts the rocket up into the air. Escape **velocity** is the speed a spacecraft needs to escape Earth's gravitational pull. It needs to be faster than 25,000 miles (40,233 km) per hour.

Weight is another problem. The heavier the rocket, the more thrust and speed it needs to lift off. For example, at its launch site, the space shuttle had one huge external tank, two solid rocket boosters, and the shuttle itself. Altogether, when the tanks were filled with fuel, they weighed 4.4 million pounds (1.99 million kilograms). That's about the same weight as 50 18-wheeler trucks!

Once a spaceship has passed the Kármán line, it can go into orbit. Going into orbit is similar to playing tug-of-war. Gravity pulls the spaceship back toward Earth, while the speed of the ship pulls it away. For orbit to happen, the speed of the rocket or satellite must be balanced with Earth's gravitational pull. Once they are in balance, the object must maintain a speed that is just slightly less than the escape velocity.

Engineers in the past managed to conquer gravity and keep spacecraft in orbit. Engineers in the present are working on ways to improve these systems. One option is called an air-breathing rocket engine. British engineer Alan Bond, along with his team at Reaction Engines, has developed an engine called the Synergistic Air Breathing Rocket Engine (SABRE). It works something like a jet engine. Instead of having to store large amounts of liquid oxygen to ignite the fuel, it takes oxygen out of the air to mix with the fuel to create thrust. This makes the spaceship lighter and works for as long as oxygen is available.

COMING DOWN TO THE GROUND

Getting a spaceship safely back to Earth has a separate set of engineering challenges. Instead of needing to overcome gravity, landing a spaceship requires stopping gravity from working too well. Gravity serves as a force to pull a spaceship back to

The *Apollo 12* command module (*shown here*) had an ablative heat shield. The places where this shield burned away are clearly visible.

Earth. However, the closer it gets to the surface, the faster it accelerates. One thing that slows it down is Earth's atmosphere. Particles in the atmosphere rub against the spacecraft, causing friction, which slows the speed of reentry. However, friction also causes intense heat—as much as 3,000 degrees Fahrenheit (1,649 degrees Celsius). Without the proper design, the spaceship would burn up as it flies through the atmosphere, the way meteors (shooting stars) do.

Engineers have learned that designing a ship with a curved, smooth surface creates a shock wave in front of the spaceship that keeps the heat some distance away from the ship itself. Although the curved design helps protect the shuttle from the worst of the heat, it is impossible to keep all the heat away from the spacecraft. For added protection, engineers have designed different types of heat shields. The shields used on the Apollo command modules were made from an **epoxy resin** and fiberglass, which burned away from the spacecraft's surface, taking the heat with it. This is called an **ablative** heat shield. From the ground, it might have looked like the command module was on fire.

Shown here is the tiled heat shield on a space shuttle.

Tragic Failures

On any kind of spaceship, even the tiniest problem can have terrible results. This became very clear in 1986 when the *Challenger* space shuttle exploded only 73 seconds after liftoff. A faulty pressure seal, called an O-ring, in one of the booster rockets caused a fuel leak. The fuel was instantly ignited by the flames coming from the rocket engines, causing the explosion.

The shuttle program was grounded for two years while NASA created better safety procedures. After that, almost two decades passed before another accident happened. In 2003, the *Columbia* space shuttle broke up in the sky during reentry, killing all seven crew members. A piece of foam insulation had broken off the main external fuel tank 81 seconds after the shuttle launched. This alone was not a problem, but NASA employees who reviewed videos of the launch after the tragedy noticed that the piece of foam had nicked the heat shield. This allowed the heat of reentry to damage the shuttle so badly that it exploded. Again the shuttle program was grounded for two years while NASA worked on its safety procedures. The space shuttle program was officially ended in 2011 because of money and safety problems.

Another kind of heat shield is called an insulating tile shield. The space shuttles used this kind of shield. Tile grids were added to the underside of the space shuttle to absorb most of the heat. They were made of silica, which is the main component of sand. Silica insulates heat so well that if a person held the edges of one of these tiles and heated the center with a blowtorch, they would not feel the heat at all. However, there have been problems with the tiles coming off the shuttles in the past.

NASA is working on a third option: an inflatable cover made of fibers and fabrics that are heat resistant. It would be light, fold up into a small space, and inflate when the spaceship goes through reentry. In addition to keeping heat away from the spacecraft, it would help the ship slow down, or decelerate, as it reenters the atmosphere so it does not crash. A spaceship does not have brakes because brakes only work against a hard

Shown here is the Soyuz capsule falling back down to Earth. When it lands, a team meets the astronaut crew to take them and any cargo back home.

surface, so they are useless in the air. NASA expects to test the device in September 2022. To make sure no humans are harmed if the device does not work as planned, it will be sent up with an unmanned satellite. After the satellite reaches outer space, the device will come back down on its own.

If this device works, it could completely change the way spacecraft land. For most of the space program's history, command modules have used parachutes to slow them down until they splashed down in the ocean. The Soyuz module still uses parachutes but lands in the desert. A few minutes before it lands, **retro-rockets** fire from the bottom of the command module, slowing it down even more. Even though the space shuttle changed the way spaceships landed by gliding back down like an airplane on a runway, most ships, such as Soyuz, still return using command modules.

The inflatable heat shield was also designed with other planets in mind. For example, Mars has a much thinner atmosphere than Earth does, but it is still enough to create friction and heat. The heavier an object is, the more heat it creates as it drops through the atmosphere, so engineers have had to deal with weight limitations on the objects they send to Mars. If the inflatable heat shield and decelerator work, it could allow them to drop heavier items on Mars, as well as on any planets with atmospheres that are as dense as Earth's.

THINK IT THROUGH

1. Why is understanding physics such an important part of space travel?
2. Can you think of any materials besides silica that could be used to insulate a space shuttle?
3. Why might the inflatable decelerator be better than a parachute?

To make sure all the astronauts stay safe, NASA carefully monitors everything from the Mission Control Center in Houston, Texas.

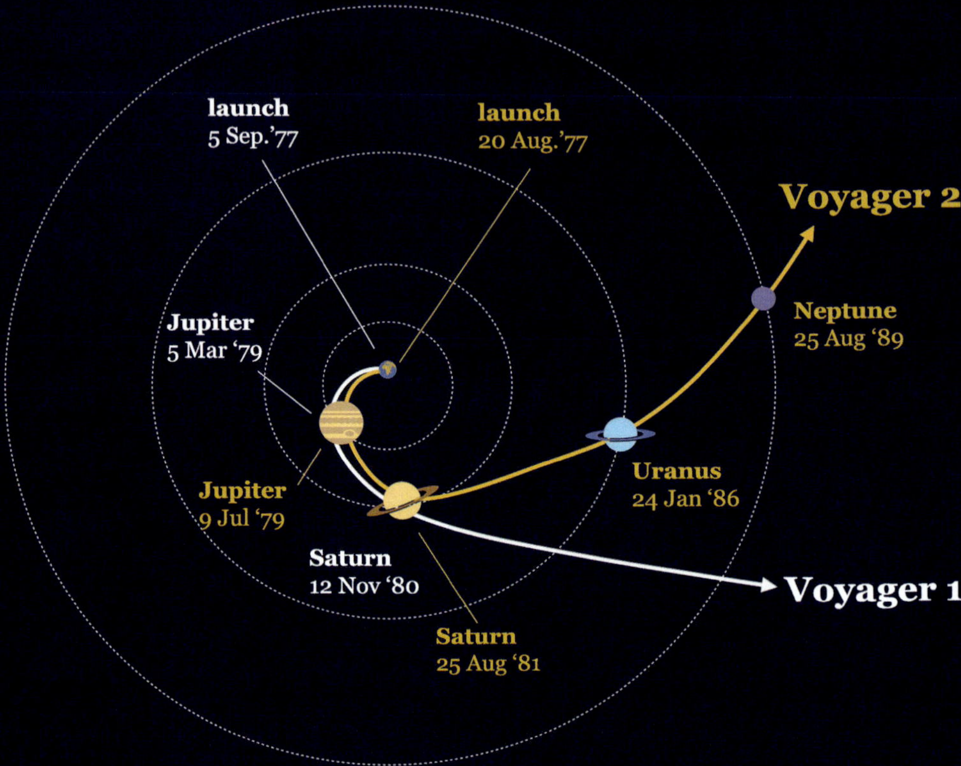

This diagram shows the paths of the Voyager probes (*below*) and the length of time it took them to reach each location.

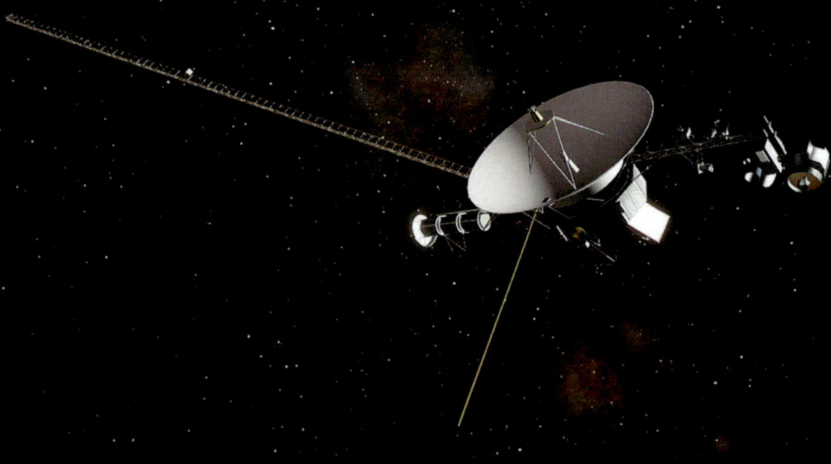

CHAPTER THREE

Moving and Protecting the Ship

After reaching orbit, a spaceship needs propulsion to travel farther. Propulsion is what pushes an object forward. Many science fiction stories involve spaceships that travel faster than the speed of light. However, although technology has changed a great deal since the first rocket engines were made, the speed at which spaceships are able to travel has remained the same. This means humans are a long way off from exploring the farthest reaches of the galaxy. It takes between seven and nine months just to reach Mars, which is the closest planet humans would be able to land on. To get out of the solar system completely, it would take hundreds of thousands of years.

One of America's unmanned **probes**, *Voyager 1*, has left our solar system and is headed out into interstellar space. However, a true starship, one that will carry astronauts or passengers to other star systems, is still a long way from becoming reality. Until engineers can find a way to increase the speed of spaceships or to place humans into **suspended animation** for extremely long voyages, manned space travel beyond our solar system will remain impossible.

USING IONS FOR FUEL

There are several different ways ships can be propelled through space. One method that has been used for several decades is ion propulsion. *Deep Space 1*, a spacecraft used from 1998 to 2001, did flybys of asteroids and comets to collect data. It was the

Shown here is an artist's recreation of *Deep Space 1*.

first to use the ion propulsion system. This type of system does not use liquid propellants the way vehicles such as the Voyager and Apollo series did. Instead, it uses gases to create thrust.

Ion propulsion works by using electricity to make negatively-charged electrons collide with the neutral atoms in the propellant, or the gas that is being used as fuel. Xenon is the most commonly used propellant because it is easy to ionize. It is also **inert** and easy to store, both of which are ideal qualities for spaceship fuel. When electrons collide with the propellant, the propellant atoms release electrons to become positively charged ions. The combination of positive ions and negative electrons balances out to become a **plasma** that has no electric charge. Magnetic fields then direct the plasma to where it is ejected from the engine, creating thrust.

Ion propulsion fuel lasts much longer than rocket fuel does, but ion propulsion cannot move a ship fast enough to achieve escape velocity. For that, we still need chemical propulsion, which is the kind of engine rockets currently use. Instead of using electricity, a chemical engine uses a chemical reaction to create thrust. A spaceship with a chemical propulsion system can get up to speed very quickly, but it is like a bullet: It keeps going in the direction it started off in and cannot slow down until it runs out of power. In contrast, an ion propulsion system

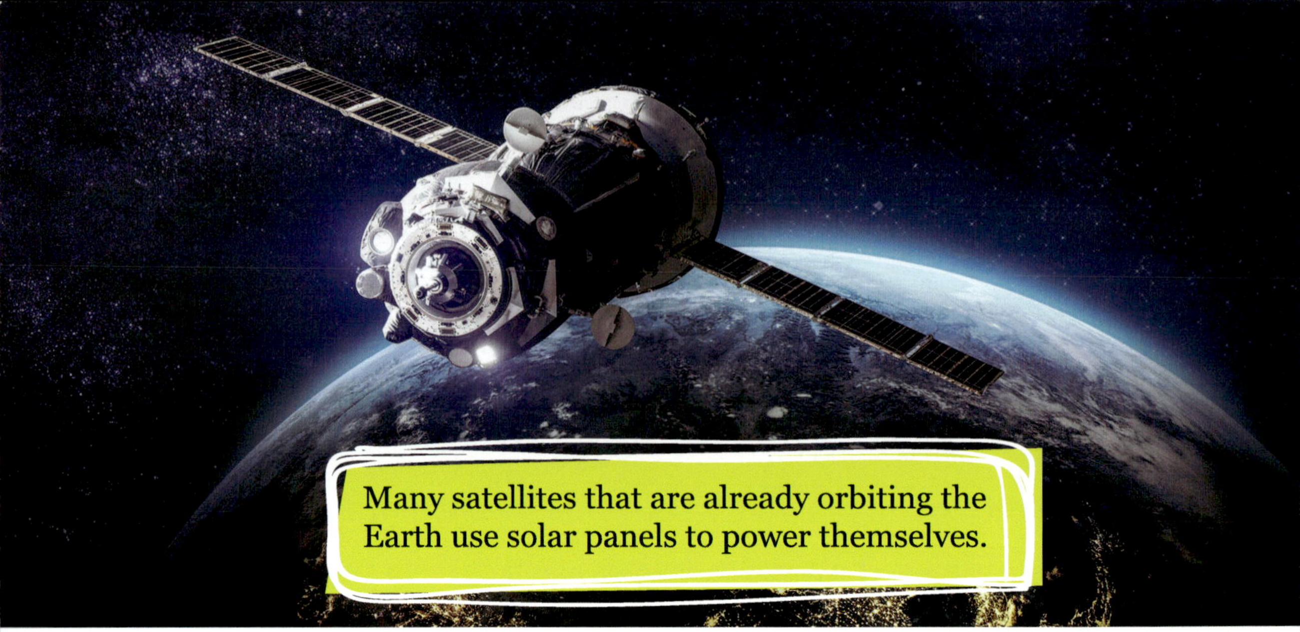

Many satellites that are already orbiting the Earth use solar panels to power themselves.

starts out slow, but it can accelerate to more than 200,000 miles (321,869 km) per hour over time. Additionally, it is easier for spaceships that use ion propulsion to turn, slow down, and stop.

Another issue with ion propulsion engines is that they require a lot of electricity to keep working. One way to solve this problem is to use solar panels to store energy from the sun in batteries on the spaceship. The batteries then send power to the engines. This is called solar electric propulsion. Another option is to use nuclear electric propulsion. It works the same way, but instead of being powered by the sun, the electricity comes from a small nuclear reactor on the spaceship.

THE NUCLEAR OPTION

Another way to use nuclear power is through nuclear thermal propulsion. Instead of using nuclear material to create electricity, this type of engine transfers heat from the spaceship's nuclear reactor to a liquid propellant. The heat turns the liquid into a gas, similar to the way boiling water turns into steam. As the propellant turns from liquid to gas, it expands and is forced out through an opening at the back of the engine to create thrust.

Nuclear thermal propulsion can move a ship much faster than ion propulsion can, and it is much more **efficient** than chemical propulsion. Additionally, like ion propulsion engines, they make it easier for a spaceship to slow or turn. Using chemical propulsion, a spaceship would have to wait to make a trip to Mars and back until the planets were lined up exactly right. This would take three years in total. Using nuclear power, a spaceship could shorten that time because it could turn in space to land in the right place. As of 2021, NASA is working on designing nuclear thermal engines, but it will be several more years before a safe and effective engine is created.

A SAILING SPACESHIP

Solar sails are another type of propulsion system that does not require a chemical propellant. Made of ultra-thin, aluminum-coated plastic, the sails are folded and wound around spools attached to flexible **booms**. The booms deploy after the spacecraft is in orbit, unfurling the sails. Solar sails work by catching the sun's light and turning it into energy. Light particles called photons do not have mass, but they do have momentum. The surface of the solar sail has a mirror-like shine, so light bounces off it. When the photons hit the sail and when they bounce off, they transfer their momentum to the sail, giving it a push. This continuing pressure causes the spacecraft to increase its speed over time.

On Earth, a vehicle needs to gain enough momentum to overcome air resistance, friction, and other forces that act on it to slow it down. In space, there is nothing to slow a spaceship down, so any momentum will move it. A nonprofit organization called the Planetary Society, headed by Bill Nye "the Science Guy," launched a solar sail-powered spacecraft, *LightSail 2*, in June 2019. It is being used to test the best ways to advance solar sailing technology. There are several benefits of using solar sails

This image shows how a solar sail would look in space.

Living in Space

The inside of a spaceship needs to be designed just as carefully as the outside. Without gravity, many things that are easy to do on Earth need special adjustments to be done in space. For example, the toilet has a strap near it that astronauts need to hang onto so they do not float away before they are done going to the bathroom. Similarly, astronauts must attach their sleeping bags to the wall or ceiling so they do not float around the room.

Water is another issue in space. The bathroom does not have a shower because the water droplets would float around instead of falling straight down as they do on Earth. For this reason, part of a spaceship's cargo includes pouches filled with liquid soap and water that astronauts can squeeze right onto their skin, as well as rinseless shampoo for their hair. Since there is no way to get more water for washing and drinking, spaceships have equipment that collects, cleans, and recycles all liquid, including sweat and urine. The ISS also needs room for exercise equipment because zero-gravity causes bone and muscle loss over time unless a person exercises for at least two hours per day.

instead of other kinds of propulsion: The power will never run out, sails are cheaper to make than engines, they can reach higher speeds over a long period of time than chemical engines, and they save space onboard because no extra fuel needs to be packed.

SHIELDS UP

The fact that there is no atmosphere in space means there is no protection for a spaceship. Radiation, extreme temperatures, and **space debris** that would normally burn up in a planet's atmosphere are all dangers to a spaceship and its crew. For this reason, choosing the right materials to make a spaceship out of is incredibly important.

Titanium is one of the metals that has been used for spacecraft. It is very strong and lightweight and can handle extreme temperatures and pressure. Kevlar—the material used in bulletproof vests—is another material that has been used for protective sheeting.

In addition to these strong materials, different types of shields are used on the outside of spaceships. The first spacecraft shield ever invented was called the Whipple shield after its inventor, Fred Whipple. It works by placing a sheet of aluminum in front of the spacecraft to act as a bumper. When space debris hits the bumper at high speed, it breaks up into smaller pieces, which do less damage. The bumper is made to be damaged instead of the spacecraft, so when the spacecraft lands on Earth, the bumper is replaced before the next flight. The Whipple shield has proven so effective that it has been in use since it was invented

NASA's *Stardust* probe has a Whipple shield. In this photo, the bumper is on the bottom.

in the 1940s. However, variations on the Whipple shield have been created over time. One is called the stuffed Whipple, which involves placing several more layers between the bumper and the spaceship wall.

Composites, or mixtures of metals, have also been developed for use in space technology. Some are made of pieces so small they can only be seen through a microscope. Making composites at this extra-small level is called nanotechnology. Because of their structure, composites such as graphene and carbon nanotubes are extremely strong but still lightweight.

An insulating material called aerogel is also used for protection from extreme temperatures. Aerogel is made by taking all the liquid from a gel and replacing it with gas. This process makes aerogel similar to a sponge, filled with tiny pockets of air, which creates an effective heat insulator for spaceships.

THINK IT THROUGH

1. Why can't an ion-propelled ship get up to escape velocity?
2. What problems might a nuclear-powered spaceship run into?
3. Why is space debris so dangerous?

NASA has sent multiple unmanned spacecraft called rovers to Mars (*shown here*). Thanks to the photos and temperature data they have taken, NASA can design future spacecraft to work well in cold, dry, rocky conditions.

CHAPTER FOUR

Looking Forward

Space technology has advanced amazingly fast in just a few decades. If it continues at this pace, humanity may be traveling across the galaxy much sooner than we ever thought possible. As of 2022, space tourism is a major field of exploration. NASA is also preparing to return to the moon to help gather enough information to make a mission to Mars possible in the future.

A TOURIST DESTINATION

Space tourism is not exactly new. A company called Space Adventures has been booking short stays on the ISS since 2000. However, these trips can cost up to $20 million. Several private companies have been testing **suborbital** and orbital ships to carry passengers into space for brief periods of time for a more reasonable cost. However, at $250,000 or more per ticket, it will still be out of reach of the average person for a long time.

Three billionaires have formed space tourism companies as of 2022. They have all been testing their ships for several years. Virgin Galactic, founded by Richard Branson, and Blue Origin, founded by Jeff Bezos, are working on suborbital space trips. Both companies use rocket-powered ships to take up to six passengers per flight into suborbit. The third company is SpaceX, founded by Elon Musk. Musk's company has been working with NASA to develop spacecraft.

THE ARTEMIS MISSION

In 1969, the *Apollo 11* spacecraft landed on the moon for the first time in human history. Today, NASA is working on getting back to the moon. The mission is called Artemis because in Greek mythology, Apollo and Artemis were twins. Apollo was the god of the sun, and Artemis was the goddess of the moon. The goal of the Artemis mission is to create a lunar base camp where robots and astronauts can stay while they conduct research and explore the moon. However, scientific research is only one reason why people want to go back

Shown here is the inside of the SpaceX *Crew Dragon* flight capsule.

to the moon. Some private companies are also looking to the moon as a new place to mine mineral resources.

There are many different parts to the Artemis mission. NASA is building a spacecraft called the *Orion*, which will carry astronauts—including the first woman and the first person of color to land on the moon—to and from lunar orbit. The *Orion* will dock at the Gateway spaceship, which is similar to the ISS, but it will orbit the moon instead of the Earth.

Orion has three parts: the service module, the crew module, and the Launch Abort System (LAS). The service module, designed by the European Space Agency, will hold the power and propulsion system. On the outside, solar panels will collect sunlight to create electricity. The middle section will hold the crew, while the LAS is designed to detach and carry the crew to safety in case of an emergency.

From Gateway, astronauts will be able to transfer to a lunar lander when they want to travel to the surface of the moon. No rocket is currently powerful enough to carry the Orion as well as its crew and cargo in one trip, so NASA is also

This image is an artist's drawing of what the *Orion* service module will look like once it is fully built.

building the space launch system (SLS) rocket. It will be the most powerful in the world when it is finished.

MISSION TO MARS

The engineers at NASA have mapped out a three-part plan for the future Mars missions. The first part, called Earth Reliant, focuses on research aboard the ISS through the mid-2020s. It will test and develop new technologies, communications, and systems for human health and protection during deep space travel.

The second section, Proving Ground, will be conducted from 2018 through 2030. All the activities planned near the moon and with Gateway will prepare astronauts for the voyages to Mars and other planets. NASA's Asteroid Redirect Mission will send a robotic spacecraft to retrieve an asteroid from space and place it in orbit around the moon. Astronauts will gather samples from the asteroid and practice spacewalking in preparation for Mars missions.

The final part, Earth Independent, is already in progress. Probes and land rovers have been transmitting information from Mars to prepare spaceships for landing and finding possible areas for astronauts to live. If the Earth Reliant phase gives scientists research they can use to solve certain problems, astronauts may be heading to Mars as early as 2030. However, if they do not have all the research and technology they need at that point, the date will be pushed back.

Other countries, as well as some private companies and organizations, also have plans to journey to Mars. China has emerged in the 21st century as a new space superpower. Its engineers have successfully established an orbiting space station, launched a spaceship to the moon, and plan to have bases on the moon and Mars by the middle of the century. In 2021, China announced that it already has manned Mars launches planned every two or three years starting from 2033.

FROM SCIENCE FICTION TO REALITY

Engineers are currently designing spaceships that may not exist until many years into the future. One of these, the Bussard ramjet, would use an enormous magnetic funnel to collect hydrogen for fuel, eliminating the need to carry fuel on the spaceship. There is a lot of hydrogen in space, so the idea makes sense. However, as of 2021, no one has been able to design a practical working Bussard ramjet.

Another concept developed by a NASA team is the Nautilus X. It uses current technology and is designed to travel through space. Though unable to land on other planets, it could

False Promises

In 2011, many people responded to an advertisement from a company called Mars One, which was looking for volunteers for a one-way trip to Mars. The idea was that these volunteers would be the first to establish a Mars colony. Mars One promised that this would take place as early as 2020. Although the company held interviews and selected participants, no further progress took place.

In 2014, two students from the Massachusetts Institute of Technology (MIT) published a paper proving that Mars One did not have enough money or the right technology to fulfill its goals on the promised timeline. The company admitted that this was true and that it was hoping more people would contribute money. In 2016, Mars One ran out of money, but its website claimed it would be able to send a crew to Mars by 2032. As of 2021, the company's website has removed the option to sign up as a crew member and acknowledged the company's lack of funds. It also suggests that although Mars One never fulfilled its goal of setting up a permanent Mars base, it was successful simply because it may have sparked the imagination of future space explorers.

serve as a docking station for landing spaceships. It would be solar-powered and provide space farms to grow food for the astronauts.

The Skylon spaceplane, invented by Alan Bond, uses the SABRE rocket engine as well as a horizontal takeoff and landing system. Resembling a sleek black torpedo, it would be completely reusable, which would greatly cut down on the cost of going to space. Bond's intention is to replace standard rocket-launch systems and create the kind of easy

This image shows what a Bussard ramjet could look like. The scoop on the front collects hydrogen atoms and turns them into fuel, which shoots out of the back to propel the spacecraft forward.

back-and-forth space travel we see in science fiction. In the future, going to space could be as commonplace as going on vacation to another country.

New heavy-duty launch systems and new technologies are also being developed. Harold White, a physicist at NASA, is even working on an idea for an engine that can reach faster-than-light speeds. However, until then, spaceships will not be able to travel fast enough to reach other solar systems in a reasonable amount of time. At the speeds spaceships can currently travel, it would take thousands of years to reach the nearest star system. Until scientists can figure out how to safely make spaceships travel faster, humans may have to be content with exploring our own solar system.

THINK IT THROUGH

1. Why do space tourists need to train before their trip?
2. Do you think space exploration should be funded by billionaires or by the government? Explain your answer.
3. What problems might need to be worked out before the Bussard ramjet can become a reality?

GLOSSARY

ablative: Relating to ablation, or the process of losing a part by melting or vaporization.

boom: A long pole attached to the bottom of a sail.

capsule: A small part of a spacecraft, separate from the rest of the spacecraft, often where people live and work.

efficient: Able to produce a desired result with little waste.

epoxy resin: A type of glue that is flexible.

inert: Not chemically reactive.

module: A part of a space vehicle that can work by itself.

plasma: Matter with many of the properties of a gas that has been subjected to an electromagnetic charge.

probe: A spacecraft designed to travel through space to record and transmit data.

retro-rockets: Rockets that fire in the opposite direction of the spacecraft's momentum to decelerate it.

space debris: Dust, small meteors, and other objects that are in orbit or floating in space.

suborbital: Flying beyond Earth's atmosphere but not reaching orbit.

suspended animation: The state of slowing down a body's life processes without causing death.

velocity: Quickness of motion in a certain direction.

FIND OUT MORE

Books

Kluger, Jeffrey, and Ruby Shamir. *To the Moon!: The True Story of the American Heroes on the Apollo 8 Spaceship*. Waterville, ME: Thorndike Press, 2018.

Morey, Allan. *Space Shuttles*. Minneapolis, MN: Bellwether Media, 2018.

Wainwright, Max. *Scratch Code: Space Tech*. New York, NY: Crabtree Publishing, 2020.

Websites

BrainPOP: Space Flight
www.brainpop.com/technology/scienceandindustry/spaceflight
Watch a short movie to learn more about the science behind space flight.

European Space Agency: ESA Kids
www.esa.int/esaKIDSen/index.html
Learn all about space and space programs.

NASA Kids' Club
www.nasa.gov/kidsclub/index.html
This interactive website includes games, information, and activities to do at home.

Organizations

NASA Headquarters
300 E. Street SW, Suite 5R30
Washington, DC 20546
www.nasa.gov
NASA can provide those interested with the newest space exploration projects, how to become an astronaut, and more.

Space Camp
US Space and Rocket Center
One Tranquility Base
Huntsville, AL 35805
www.spacecamp.com
Spend between two days and a week training like an astronaut.

Virginia Air & Space Science Center
600 Settlers Landing Road
Hampton, VA 23669
vasc.org
This museum and educational center is the place where NASA first started its space exploration. It contains several real spacecraft, including the *Apollo 12* command module.

Publisher's note to educators and parents: Our editors have carefully reviewed these websites to ensure that they are suitable for students. Many websites change frequently, however, and we cannot guarantee that a site's future contents will continue to meet our high standards of quality and educational value. Be advised that students should be closely supervised whenever they access the Internet.

INDEX

ABOUT THE AUTHOR

SOPHIE WASHBURNE has been a freelance writer and editor of young adult and adult books for more than 10 years. She travels extensively with her husband, Alan. When they are not traveling, they live in Wales with their cat, Zoe. Sophie enjoys doing crafts and cooking when she has spare time. She would like to thank Jenna Curry for her invaluable contributions to this book.